Let's Celebrate Christmas

Kathleen Clark

MOORLEY'S Print & Publishing

COPYRIGHT

We do not ask for any "performing rights" royalties, but remind you that it is illegal to reproduce in print, by typing, writing or photocopying, any part of this publication without the Publisher's written permission.

No permission is needed however, to use this material, as part of an act of worship or a Christmas programme providing that copyright obligations, as listed above, are fulfilled.

ISBN 0 86071 261 3

MOORLEY'S Print & Publishing
23 Park Rd., Ilkeston, Derbys DE7 5DA
Tel/Fax: (0115) 932 0643

*For May Thompson
of Aldersgate Methodist Church, Low Moor,
under whose influence so many young people
learnt to cherish Christian values.*

Author's Note: This Carol Service was successfully used by me with children aged seven to fifteen. As a teacher in charge of Religious Education and a writer I wanted to convey the Christian message in as many fresh and interesting ways as I could.

A CHILDREN'S CAROL SERVICE

ALL: Once In Royal David's City.
Reading: The First Christmas Card.
Distribution of Christmas Cards to members of the congregation.

ALL: The First Nowell.
Reading: The First Mince Pie.

ALL: Still the Night, Holy the Night.
Reading: The First Christmas Tree.

ALL: The Holly and the Ivy.
Reading: The First Christmas Pudding.

ALL: Unto Us A Boy Is Born.
Reading: Christmas Customs.

ALL: Away In A Manger.
Reading: The Animals At Christmas.

ALL: The Rocking Carol.
(This may be sung by a children's choir.)
Reading: The Rocking Ceremony.

ALL: O Little Town Of Bethlehem
Reading: St. Luke, chapter 2 vs. 1-16.

ALL: Oh Come All Ye Faithful.
Reading: Christmas Message.

The Benediction.

These nine readings may be interspersed with items by the choir, recorders, percussion band, etc.

Reading 1:

THE FIRST CHRISTMAS CARD

When was the first Christmas Card sent? You don't know. Well the actual date is uncertain but a card designed by a boy of sixteen called William Egley and now in the British Museum was believed to have been sent in 1842.

In 1844 Rev. Edward Bradley of Newcastle and William Dobson of Birmingham sent hand-painted cards to save themselves the trouble of writing letters at Christmas time. Then J. C. Horsley, an artist, designed a card with a Christmas greeting on it in 1846 and about a thousand were sold. By 1870 the custom was well established.

The original cards all had something to do with the birth of Christ. It is a great pity that we tend to forget this and send pictures of puppies, kittens and all manner of things that have nothing to do with Christmas. Perhaps we, as Christian boys and girls, could remember this and do something to put Christ back into Christmas.

Reading 2:

THE FIRST MINCE PIES

Have you made your Mince Pies yet? Perhaps you think this is a strange question to ask in a carol service. Not so. Did you know that the first Mince Pies were oblong shaped like a manger? At first they were filled with minced meat, but later fruit and peel were added and the colours reminded people of gold, frankincense and myrrh. Later still a top was added to represent the roof of the stable and the hole which allows the steam to escape was star-shaped. So as you wish people a happy Christmas and offer them a Mince Pie spare a thought for Jesus whose birthday you are celebrating.

Reading 3:

THE FIRST CHRISTMAS TREE

Have you a Christmas Tree at home? Did you know that such trees were practically unknown in this country until the middle of the last century. It is true that a certain German merchant wrote in 1605, "At Christmas they set up fir trees in the houses at Strasbourg and hang on them roses cut out of many-coloured papers, apples, wafers, gold foil, sweets, etc." but it was not until Prince Albert ordered a Christmas Tree for Windsor Castle in 1841 that the custom became popular in this country.

If you have wondered just why we use a fir tree listen to this old German legend. A very holy man St. Boniface, who lived in the eighth century was sent from England to Germany to preach about Jesus. On a frosty night in December he was walking in a wood when he came across a group of people worshipping a pagan god. This was the night when offerings were to be made to this god and they were met beneath an oak tree to offer a human sacrifice of a little boy. Just as they were leading him forward St. Boniface snatched an axe and felled the great tree with a single stroke. As it fell to the ground it left behind a little fir tree which had been growing between its roots.

The Saint turned to the people and said, "From this night that little tree shall be your holy emblem.

It is the wood of peace for your houses are built of it. It is the sign of eternal life for its leaves are evergreen. It points to Heaven and shall henceforth be called the tree of the Christ-child. See that you do not forget."

Reading 4:

THE FIRST CHRISTMAS PUDDING

I wonder what you have put into your Christmas Puddings this year. The first one which was made around 1670 might have surprised you. It was just stiff porridge with raisins added. Then meat broth, chopped sheeps' tongues, fruit juice, wine, spice and breadcrumbs were mixed together and this was served in a semi-liquid state. Not much like the delicious dish covered with custard or rum sauce we are used to today.

Do you put a sprig of holly on the top? In Norway and Sweden it is known as the Christ-thorn because the prickly leaves are like the thorns in the crown that Jesus was forced to wear on Good Friday and the red berries remind us of the drops of blood that came when the thorns pierced His flesh. So once again a popular custom reminds us of Him.

Reading 5:

CHRISTMAS CUSTOMS

Have you ever kissed anybody under the Mistletoe? I wonder if you know the significance of your action.

Let this legend explain. Balder, the sun god, was much loved by all the other gods who protected him by placing spells on everything that might harm him. Water could not drown him, swords could not hurt him and poison had no effect on him. Unfortunately they forgot to place a spell on Mistletoe. Loki, the god of evil, discovered this. Making an arrow out of a Mistletoe branch, he put it in the bow of Hoder the blind god and Balder was killed. The other gods brought him back to life and the Mistletoe promised never to hurt anybody again. It became an emblem of love and when we kiss under it we should remember this.

Many children in the world this Christmas-time will not have the strength to follow their own Christmas customs. They are starving. Let us pray for them in love and do what we can to help them by giving money or time to make sure that they will live to see many more Christmases.

Reading 6:

THE ANIMALS AT CHRISTMAS

Christian man has never forgotten that the animals, some of whom shared the Bethlehem stable, bear an honoured place in the Christmas celebrations.

In Poland where there is a fast on Christmas Eve the master of the house waits for the first star to appear before he distributes small pieces of unleavened bread to every member of the family and carries some to the horses and cattle in the outbuildings. Then everyone sits down to a table on which a white cloth covers a layer of straw or hay in memory of Christ's birth in a stable.

In some houses a wheatsheaf stands in a corner of the room and later these sheaves are taken into the fields where they serve as a charm to ensure a good fruit harvest and a feast for the birds. Cattle and horses are given extra rations and in other parts of the country people carry wheat to church on Christmas morning and then give it to any chickens and birds they may see on their way home.

In Sweden a sheaf of corn is sometimes fixed to a high pole for the birds while in Finland special cakes are made and fastened on to the stable roofs perhaps because in the 13th century St. Francis said that animals should be included in the rejoicings "for the reverence of the Son of God whom on such a night the most blessed Virgin Mary did lay down in the stall between the ox and the ass."

Reading 7:

THE ROCKING CEREMONY

In some out-of-the-way villages in Bavaria the people will, on Christmas Eve, take part in the Rocking Ceremony. A special part of the house is set aside for the Christmas Crib. Some are big and expensive, some small and home-made just like you can make for yourselves. Half-an-hour before midnight the whole family - even the tiniest toddler - will get ready for the feast that is to come. First they must line up behind father as he sings the Rocking Carol and gently rocks the Christ Child's Cradle. Next, mother takes her turn and they go on until even the toddler has looked on the model of Baby Jesus and listened to the words of the carol. "We will give you coat of fur. We will rock you, rock you, rock you. We will help you all we can. Darling, darling, little man."

Reading 8:

ST. LUKE, CHAPTER 2: VERSES 1-16.

Section 9:

NOTE: If the Church or School already has a Christmas Crib this section can take place with the children kneeling round it. Alternatively a large Cross made from two pieces of wood covered with silver foil can form a centre piece or the section may be performed without any stage properties. The characters are either the nine readers used so far or nine new children if a larger cast is desired.

1ST READER: Now we come to the real message of Christmas. It is very simple. God wants us to realise that it is more blessed to give than to receive. We give thanks for people who remember this all the year round.

2ND READER: Thankyou to parents who work hard to provide us with food and shelter.

3rd READER: Thankyou to doctors and nurses for their skill and patience.

4TH READER: Thankyou to people who raise money to feed the hungry.

5TH READER: Thankyou for friends and friendship.

6TH READER: Thankyou to those who make others feel wanted in orphanages and old people's homes.

7TH READER: Thankyou for everyone who is working to bring peace to the world.

8TH READER: Thankyou God for the greatest gift of all - your son Jesus Christ.

9TH READER: A or B will sing a new carol which shows how children too can play their part.

CAROL: "I Wonder" can be sung to the tune of 'While Shepherds Watched Their Flocks By Night' or any suitable 8.6.8.6. tune.

* MINISTER OR LEADER: Now the children have told us so much about Christmas, let us, as we sing the carol 'Oh Come All Ye Faithful' be thinking of what we can do to make the world a better place in the coming year.

BENEDICTION.

---

* If used in a Church Service this would be the appropriate time for a short address, if desired, to emphasise the true meaning of Christmas.

- 14 -

I WONDER

I wonder if at Bethlehem
Before the day was done
The little children brought their gifts
   For Mary's baby son.

I wonder if they touched His hand
And stroked His downy head
I wonder if they smoothed the hay
   That lined His manger bed.

I wonder if they watched the Kings
Bring jewels rich and rare
And saw the shepherds bring a lamb
   I wish that I'd been there.

For though I'm only just a child
Yet I would do my part
And give to Jesus all He asks
   A helpful, loving heart.

                Kathleen M. Clark.

MOORLEY'S are growing Publishers, adding several new titles to our list each year. We also undertake private publications and commissioned works.

Our range of publications includes: **Books of Verse**
- Devotional Poetry
- Recitations

Drama
- Bible Plays
- Sketches
- Nativity Plays
- Passiontide Plays
- Easter Plays
- Demonstrations

Resource Books
- Assembly Material
- Songs & Musicals
- Children's Addresses
- Prayers & Graces
- Daily Readings
- Books for Speakers

Activity Books
- Quizzes
- Puzzles
- Painting Books

Daily Readings

Church Stationery
- Notice Books
- Cradle Rolls
- Hymn Board Numbers

Please send a S.A.E. (approx 9" x 6") for the current catalogue or consult your local Christian Bookshop who should stock or be able to order our titles.